SELECTIONS FROM
SARA TEASDALE

Sara Teasdale for Children

SARA TEASDALE

This collection published 2020
by Living Book Press
Copyright © Living Book Press, 2020

ISBN: 978-1-922348-20-3

All rights reserved. No part of this publication may be reproduced, stored in a retrieval system, or transmitted in any other form or means – electronic, mechanical, photocopying, recording or otherwise, without the prior permission of the copyright owner and the publisher or as provided by Australian law.

A catalogue record for this book is available from the National Library of Australia

CONTENTS

from Sonnets to Duse

The Love that Goes A-begging	1
Wishes	2
Dusk in Autumn	4
Dream Song	5
Faults	6

from Helen of Troy and Other Poems

Snow Song	7
November	8
A Winter Night	9
Dawn	10
Dusk	11
Rain at Night	12
Christmas Carol	13
A Ballad of Two Knights	14
The Faery Forest	15
A Minuet of Mozart's	16
Twilight	17
Grandfather's Love	18
The Kind Moon	19
Spring Night	20

from Rivers to the Sea

April	21
Moods	22
A Winter Blue Jay	23
In the Train	24
Morning	25
May Night	26
Dusk in June	27
The Sea Wind	28
The Cloud	29
Twilight	30
The Star	31
In the Carpenter's Shop	32
Swallow Flight	33
Thoughts	34
To Dick on his Sixth Birthday	35
The River	36
To Rose	37

Night in Arizona	38
Vignettes Overseas: Stresa	39
Vignettes Overseas: Florence	40
Vignettes Overseas: Hamburg	41

from Love Songs

Barter	42

from Flame and Shadow

Stars	43
The Coin	44
Redbirds	45
"Only in Sleep"	46
Lost Things	47
"My Heart Is Heavy"	48
May Day	49
Thoughts	50

from Dark of the Moon

February Twilight	51
A December Day	52
Autumn Dusk	53
In the Wood	54

from Stars To-night: Verses for Boys and Girls

Night	55
Late October	56
The Falling Star	57
The Spicebush in March	58
Calm Morning at Sea	59
To Arcturus Returning	60
A June Day	61
Rhyme of November Stars	62
I Stood Upon a Star	63
Winter Noon	64

from Strange Victory

Moon's Ending	65
Autumn on the Beaches	66
Age	67
In a Darkening Garden	68
In Memory of Vachel Lindsay	69
Grace Before Sleep	70
Lines	71
"There Will Be Rest"	72

In selecting these poems I have tried to ensure that all are suitable for children. Sara Teasdale felt very deeply, and many of her poems reflect those feelings. Feelings of every emotion, of love, of loss, of beauty, of hopelessness, of loneliness and awe. Some of the following poems have had verses removed so that we can share these beautiful poems with our children while not having to explain some of the more adult emotions referenced later in the poem.

I hope you and your children enjoy them as much as we have.

THE PUBLISHER

THE LOVE THAT GOES A-BEGGING

Oh Loves there are that enter in,
And Loves there are that wait,
And Loves that sit a-weeping
Whose joy will come too late.

For some there be that ope their doors,
And some there be that close,
And Love must go a-begging,
But whither, no one knows.

His feet are on the thorny ways,
And on the dew-cold grass,
No ears have ever heard him sing,
No eyes have seen him pass.

And yet he wanders through the world
And makes the meadows sweet,
For all his tears and weariness
Have flowered beneath his feet.

The little purple violet
Has marked his wanderings,
And in the wind among the trees,
You hear the song he sings.

WISHES

I wish for such a lot of things
That never will come true—
And yet I want them all so much
I think they might, don't you?

I want a little kitty-cat
That's soft and tame and sweet,
And every day I watch and hope
I'll find one in the street.

But nursie says, "Come, walk along,
"Don't stand and stare like that"—
I'm only looking hard and hard
To try to find my cat.

And then I want a blue balloon
That tries to fly away,
I thought if I wished hard enough
That it would come some day.

One time when I was in the park
I knew that it would be
Beside the big old clock at home
A-waiting there for me—

And soon as we got home again,
I hurried through the hall,
And looked beside the big old clock—
It wasn't there at all.

I think I'll never wish again—
But then, what shall I do?
The wishes are a lot of fun
Although they don't come true.

DUSK IN AUTUMN

The moon is like a scimitar,
A little silver scimitar,
A-drifting down the sky.
And near beside it is a star,
A timid twinkling golden star,
That watches like an eye.

And thro' the nursery window-pane
The witches have a fire again,
Just like the ones we make,—
And now I know they're having tea,
I wish they'd give a cup to me,
With witches' currant cake.

DREAM SONG

I plucked a snow-drop in the spring,
And in my hand too closely pressed;
The warmth had hurt the tender thing,
I grieved to see it withering.

I gave my love a poppy red,
And laid it on her snow-cold breast;
But poppies need a warmer bed,
We wept to find the flower was dead.

FAULTS

They came to tell your faults to me,
They named them over one by one;
I laughed aloud when they were done,
I knew them all so well before, —
Oh, they were blind, too blind to see
Your faults had made me love you more.

SNOW SONG

Fairy snow, fairy snow,
Blowing, blowing everywhere,
Would that I
Too, could fly
Lightly, lightly through the air.

NOVEMBER

The world is tired, the year is old,
    The little leaves are glad to die,
The wind goes shivering with cold
    Among the rushes dry.

A WINTER NIGHT

My window-pane is starred with frost,
    The world is bitter cold to-night,
The moon is cruel and the wind
    Is like a two-edged sword to smite.

God pity all the homeless ones,
    The beggars pacing to and fro.
God pity all the poor to-night
    Who walk the lamp-lit streets of snow.

My room is like a bit of June,
    Warm and close-curtained fold on fold.
But somewhere, like a homeless child.
    My heart is crying in the cold.

DAWN

The greenish sky glows up in misty reds,
    The purple shadows turn to brick and stone,
The dreams wear thin, men turn upon their beds,
    And hear the milk-cart jangle by alone.

DUSK

The city's street, a roaring blackened stream
    Walled in by granite, through whose thousand eyes
A thousand yellow lights begin to gleam,
    And over all the pale, untroubled skies.

RAIN AT NIGHT

The street-lamps shine in a yellow line
    Down the splashy, gleaming street,
And the rain is heard now loud now blurred
    By the tread of homing feet.

CHRISTMAS CAROL

The kings they came from out the south.
    All dressed in ermine fine;
They bore Him gold and chrysoprase.
    And gifts of precious wine.

The shepherds came from out the north.
    Their coats were brown and old;
They brought Him little new-born lambs—
    They had not any gold.

The wise men came from out the east.
    And they were wrapped in white;
The star that led them all the way
    Did glorify the night.

The angels came from heaven high.
    And they were clad with wings;
And lo, they brought a joyful song
    The host of heaven sings.
The kings they knocked upon the door,
    The wise men entered in,
The shepherds followed after them
    To hear the song begin.

The angels sang through all the night
    Until the rising sun,
But little Jesus fell asleep
    Before the song was done.

A BALLAD OF TWO KNIGHTS

Two knights rode forth at early dawn
    A-seeking maids to wed,
Said one, "My lady must be fair,
    With gold hair on her head."

Then spake the other knight-at-arms:
    "I care not for her face,
But she I love must be a dove
    For purity and grace."

And each knight blew upon his horn
    And went his separate way,
And each knight found a lady-love
    Before the fall of day.

But she was brown who should have had
    The shining yellow hair —
I ween the knights forgot their words
    Or else they ceased to care.

THE FAERY FOREST

The faery forest glimmered
    Beneath an ivory moon,
The silver grasses shimmered
    Against a faery tune.

Beneath the silken silence
    The crystal branches slept,
And dreaming through the dew-fall
    The cold white blossoms wept.

A MINUET OF MOZART'S

Across the dimly lighted room
    The violin drew wefts of sound,
Airily they wove and wound
    And glimmered gold against the gloom.

I watched the music turn to light,
    But at the pausing of the bow,
The web was broken and the glow
    Was drowned within the wave of night.

TWILIGHT

Dreamily over the roofs
    The cold spring rain is falling,
Out in the lonely tree
    A bird is calling, calling.

Slowly over the earth
    The wings of night are falling;
My heart like the bird in the tree
    Is calling, calling, calling.

GRANDFATHER'S LOVE

They said he sent his love to me,
    They wouldn't put it in my hand,
And when I asked them where it was
    They said I couldn't understand.

I thought they must have hidden it,
    I hunted for it all the day,
And when I told them so at night
    They smiled and turned their heads away.

They say that love is something kind,
    That I can never see or touch.
I wish he'd sent me something else,
    I like his cough-drops twice as much.

THE KIND MOON

I think the moon is very kind
    To take such trouble just for me.
He came along with me from home
    To keep me company.

He went as fast as I could run;
    I wonder how he crossed the sky?
I'm sure he hasn't legs and feet
    Or any wings to fly.

Yet here he is above their roof;
    Perhaps he thinks it isn't right
For me to go so far alone,
    Though mother said I might.

SPRING NIGHT

The park is filled with night and fog,
    The veils are drawn about the world,
The drowsy lights along the paths
    Are dim and pearled.

Gold and gleaming the empty streets,
    Gold and gleaming the misty lake,
The mirrored lights like sunken swords,
    Glimmer and shake.

Oh, is it not enough to be
Here with this beauty over me?
My throat should ache with praise, and I
Should kneel in joy beneath the sky.
Oh, beauty are you not enough?

APRIL

The roofs are shining from the rain,
    The sparrows twitter as they fly,
And with a windy April grace
    The little clouds go by.

Yet the back yards are bare and brown
    With only one unchanging tree-
I could not be so sure of Spring
    Save that it sings in me.

MOODS

I am the still rain falling.
Too tired for singing mirth—
    Oh, be the green fields calling,
Oh, be for me the earth!

I am the brown bird pining
    To leave the nest and fly—
Oh, he the fresh cloud shining,
    Oh, he for me the sky!

A WINTER BLUE JAY

Crisply the bright snow whispered,
Crunching beneath our feet;
Behind us as we walked along the parkway,
Our shadows danced,
Fantastic shapes in vivid blue.
Across the lake the skaters
Flew to and fro,
With sharp turns weaving
A frail invisible net.
In ecstasy the earth
Drank the silver sunlight;
In ecstasy the skaters
Drank the wine of speed;
In ecstasy we laughed
Drinking the wine of love.
Had not the music of our joy
Sounded its highest note?
But no,
For suddenly, with lifted eyes you said,
"Oh look!"
There, on the black bough of a snow flecked maple,
Fearless and gay as our love,
A bluejay cocked his crest!
Oh who can tell the range of joy
Or set the bounds of beauty?

IN THE TRAIN

Fields beneath a quilt of snow
    From which the rocks and stubble sleep,
And in the west a shy white star
    That shivers as it wakes from deep.

The restless rumble of the train,
    The drowsy people in the car,
Steel blue twilight in the world,
    And in my heart a timid star.

MORNING

I went out on an April morning
    All alone, for my heart was high,
I was a child of the shining meadow,
    I was a sister of the sky.

There in the windy flood of morning
    Longing lifted its weight from me,
Lost as a sob in the midst of cheering,
    Swept as a sea-bird out to sea.

MAY NIGHT

The spring is fresh and fearless
    And every leaf is new,
The world is brimmed with moonlight,
    The lilac brimmed with dew.

Here in the moving shadows
    I catch my breath and sing
My heart is fresh and fearless
    And over-brimmed with spring.

DUSK IN JUNE

Evening, and all the birds
    In a chorus of shimmering sound
Are easing their hearts of joy
    For miles around.

The air is blue and sweet,
    The few first stars are white,
Oh let me like the birds
    Sing before night.

THE SEA WIND

I am a pool in a peaceful place,
I greet the great sky face to face,
I know the stars and the stately moon
And the wind that runs with rippling shoon—
But why does it always bring to me
The far-off, beautiful sound of the sea?

The marsh-grass weaves me a wall of green,
But the wind comes whispering in between,
In the dead of night when the sky is deep
The wind comes waking me out of sleep—
Why does it always bring to me
The far-off, terrible call of the sea?

THE CLOUD

I am a cloud in the heaven's height,
The stars are lit for my delight,
Tireless and changeful, swift and free,
I cast my shadow on hill and sea
But why do the pines on the mountain's crest
Call to me always, "Rest, rest"?

I throw my mantle over the moon
And I blind the sun on his throne at noon,
Nothing can tame me, nothing can bind,
I am a child of the heartless wind
But oh the pines on the mountain's crest
Whispering always, "Rest, rest."

TWILIGHT

The stately tragedy of dusk
    Drew to its perfect close,
The virginal white evening star
    Sank, and the red moon rose.

THE STAR

A white star born in the evening glow
Looked to the round green world below,
And saw a pool in a wooded place
That held like a jewel her mirrored face.
She said to the pool: "Oh, wondrous deep,
I love you, I give you my light to keep.
Oh, more profound than the moving sea
That never has shown myself to me!
Oh, fathomless as the sky is far,
Hold forever your tremulous star!"

But out of the woods as night grew cool
A brown pig came to the little pool;
It grunted and splashed and waded in
And the deepest place but reached its chin.
The water gurgled with tender glee
And the mud churned up in it turbidly.
The star grew pale and hid her face
In a bit of floating cloud like lace.

IN THE CARPENTER'S SHOP

Mary sat in the corner dreaming,
    Dim was the room and low,
While in the dusk, the saw went screaming
    To and fro.

Jesus and Joseph toiled together,
    Mary was watching them,
Thinking of kings in the wintry weather
    At Bethlehem.

Mary sat in the corner thinking,
    Jesus had grown a man;
One by one her hopes were sinking
    As the years ran.

Jesus and Joseph toiled together,
    Mary's thoughts were far
Angels sang in the wintry weather
    Under a star.

Mary sat in the corner weeping,
    Bitter and hot her tears
Little faith were the angels keeping
    All the years.

SWALLOW FLIGHT

I love my hour of wind and light,
    I love men's faces and their eyes,
I love my spirit's veering flight
    Like swallows under evening skies.

THOUGHTS

When I can make my thoughts come forth
    To walk like ladies up and down,
Each one puts on before the glass
    Her most becoming hat and gown.

But oh, the shy and eager thoughts
    That hide and will not get them dressed,
Why is it that they always seem
    So much more lovely than the rest?

TO DICK ON HIS SIXTH BIRTHDAY

Tho' I am very old and wise,
And you are neither wise nor old,
When I look far into your eyes,
I know things I was never told:
I know how flame must strain and fret
Prisoned in a mortal net;
How joy with over-eager wings,
Bruises the small heart where he sings;
How too much life, like too much gold,
Is sometimes very hard to hold...

All that is talking but I know
This much is true, six years ago
An angel living near the moon
Walked thru the sky and sang a tune
Plucking stars to make his crown
And suddenly two stars fell down,
Two falling arrows made of light.
Six years ago this very night
I saw them fall and wondered why
The angel dropped them from the sky
But when I saw your eyes I knew
The angel sent the stars to you.

THE RIVER

I came from the sunny valleys
    And sought for the open sea.
For I thought in its gray expanses
    My peace would come to me.

I came at last to the ocean
    And found it wild and black.
And I cried to the windless valleys,
    "Be kind and take me back!"

But the thirsty tide ran inland,
    And the salt waves drank of me,
And I who was fresh as the rainfall
    Am bitter as the sea.

TO ROSE

Rose, when I remember you,
Little lady, scarcely two,
I am suddenly aware
Of the angels in the air.
All your softly gracious ways
Make an island in my days
Where my thoughts fly back to be
Sheltered from too strong a sea.
All your luminous delight
Shines before me in the night
When I grope for sleep and find
Only shadows in my mind.

Rose, when I remember you,
White and glowing, pink and new,
With so swift a sense of fun
Altho' life has just begun;
With so sure a pride of place
In your very infant face,
I should like to make a prayer
To the angels in the air:
"If an angel ever brings
Me a baby in her wings,
Please be certain that it grows
Very, very much like Rose."

NIGHT IN ARIZONA

The moon is a charring ember
    Dying into the dark;
Off in the crouching mountains
    Coyotes bark.

The stars are heavy in heaven,
    Too great for the sky to hold—
What if they fell and shattered
    The earth with gold?

No lights are over the mesa,
    The wind is hard and wild,
I stand at the darkened window
    And cry like a child.

VIGNETTES OVERSEAS: STRESA

The moon grows out of the hills
    A yellow flower,
The lake is a dreamy bride
    Who waits her hour.

Beauty has filled my heart,
    It can hold no more,
It is full, as the lake is full,
    From shore to shore.

VIGNETTES OVERSEAS: FLORENCE

The bells ring over the Arno,
    Midnight, the long, long chime;
Here in the quivering darkness
    I am afraid of time.

Oh, gray bells cease your tolling.
    Time takes too much from me.
And yet to rock and river
    He gives eternity.

VIGNETTES OVERSEAS: HAMBURG

The day that I come home.
    What will you find to say,—
Words as light as foam
    With laughter light as spray?

Yet say what words you will
    The day that I come home;
I shall hear the whole deep ocean
    Beating under the foam.

BARTER

Life has loveliness to sell
    All beautiful and splendid things,
Blue waves whitened on a cliff,
    Soaring fire that sways and sings,
And children's faces looking up
Holding wonder like a cup.

Life has loveliness to sell,
    Music like a curve of gold,
Scent of pine trees in the rain,
    Eyes that love you, arms that hold,
And for your spirit's still delight,
Holy thoughts that star the night.

Spend all you have for loveliness,
    Buy it and never count the cost;
For one white singing hour of peace
    Count many a year of strife well lost,
And for a breath of ecstasy
Give all you have been, or could be.

STARS

Alone in the night
    On a dark hill
With pines around me
    Spicy and still,

And a heaven full of stars
    Over my head,
White and topaz
    And a misty red;

Myriads with beating
    Hearts of fire
That aeons
    Cannot vex or tire;

Up the dome of heaven
    Like a great hill,
I watch them marching
    Stately and still,

And I know that I
    Am honored to be
Witness
    Of so much majesty.

THE COIN

Into my heart's treasury
    I slipped a coin
That time cannot take
    Nor a thief purloin,—
Oh, better than the minting
    Of a gold-crowned king
Is the safe-kept memory
    Of a lovely thing.

REDBIRDS

Redbirds, redbirds,
    Long and long ago,
What a honey-call you had
    In hills I used to know;

Redbud, buckberry.
    Wild plum-tree
And proud river sweeping
    Southward to the sea,

Brown and gold in the sun
    Sparkling far below,
Trailing stately round her bluffs
    Where the poplars grow—

Redbirds, redbirds.
    Are you singing still
As you sang one May day
    On Saxton's Hill?

"ONLY IN SLEEP"

Only in sleep I see their faces.
    Children I played with when I was a child,
Louise comes back with her brown hair braided,
    Annie with ringlets warm and wild.

Only in sleep Time is forgotten—
    What may have come to them, who can know?
    Yet we played last night as long ago.
And the doll-house stood at the turn of the stair.

The years had not sharpened their smooth round faces,
    I met their eyes and found them mild—
Do they, too, dream of me, I wonder.
    And for them am I, too, a child?

LOST THINGS

Oh, I could let the world go by,
    Its loud new wonders and its wars,
But how will I give up the sky
    When winter dusk is set with stars?

And I could let the cities go.
    Their changing customs and their creeds,—
But oh, the summer rains that blow
    In silver on the jewel-weeds!

"MY HEART IS HEAVY"

My heart is heavy with many a song
    Like ripe fruit hearing down the tree,
But I can never give you one—
    My songs do not belong to me.

Yet in the evening, in the dusk
    When moths go to and fro.
In the gray hour if the fruit has fallen.
    Take it, no one will know.

MAY DAY

A delicate fabric of bird song
    Floats in the air,
The smell of wet wild earth
    Is everywhere.

Red small leaves of the maple
    Are clenched like a hand,
Like girls at their first communion
    The pear trees stand.

Oh I must pass nothing by
    Without loving it much,
The raindrop try with my lips,
    The grass with my touch;

For how can I be sure
    I shall see again
The world on the first of May
    Shining after the rain?

THOUGHTS

When I am all alone
    Envy me most,
Then my thoughts flutter round me
    In a glimmering host;

Some dressed in silver,
    Some dressed in white,
Each like a taper
    Blossoming light;

Most of them merry,
    Some of them grave,
Each of them lithe
    As willows that wave;

Some bearing violets,
    Some bearing bay,
One with a burning rose
    Hidden away—

When I am all alone
    Envy me then,
For I have better friends
    Than women and men.

FEBRUARY TWILIGHT

I stood beside a hill
    Smooth with new-laid snow,
A single star looked out
    From the cold evening glow.

There was no other creature
    That saw what I could see—
I stood and watched the evening star
    As long as it watched me.

A DECEMBER DAY

Dawn turned on her purple pillow
    And late, late came the winter day.
Snow was curved to the boughs of the willow.
    The sunless world was white and gray.

At noon we heard a blue jay scolding.
    At five the last thin light was lost
From snow-banked windows faintly holding
    The feathery filigree of frost.

AUTUMN DUSK

I saw above a sea of hills
    A solitary planet shine.
And there was no one near or far
    To keep the world from being mine.

IN THE WOOD

I heard the water-fall rejoice
    Singing like a choir,
I saw the sun flash out of it
    Azure and amber fire.

The earth was like an open flower
    Enamelled and arrayed,
The path I took to find its heart
    Fluttered with sun and shade.

And while earth lured me, gently, gently,
    Happy and all alone,
Suddenly a heavy snake
    Reared black upon a stone.

NIGHT

Stars over snow
    And in the west a planet
Swinging below a star —
    Look for a lovely thing and you will find it,
It is not far —
    It never will be far.

LATE OCTOBER

I found ten kinds of wild flowers growing
On a steely day that looked like snowing:
Queen Anne's lace, and blue heal-all,
A buttercup, straggling, grown too tall,
A rusty aster, a chicory flower —
Ten I found in half an hour.
The air was blurred with dry leaves flying.
Gold and scarlet, gaily dying.
A squirrel ran off with a nut in his mouth.
And always, always, flying south.
Twittering, the birds went by
Flickering sharp against the sky.
Some in great bows, some in wedges.
Some in bands with wavering edges;
Flocks and flocks were flying over
With the north wind for their drover.
"Flowers," I said, "you'd better go.
Surely it's coming on for snow," —
They did not heed me, nor heed the birds.
Twittering thin, far-fallen words —
The others thought of to-morrow, but they
Only remembered yesterday.

THE FALLING STAR

I saw a star slide down the sky,
Blinding the north as it went by,
Too burning and too quick to hold.
Too lovely to be bought or sold.
Good only to make wishes on
And then forever to be gone.

THE SPICEBUSH IN MARCH

Spicebush, yellow spicebush, tell me
    Where you found so much clear gold?
Every branch and every twig
    Has as much as it can hold.
Flaunting before tattered winter
    Your new dress the wind whips round —
Color, color! You were first.
    You dredged and drew it from the ground!

CALM MORNING AT SEA

Midocean like a pale blue morning-glory
    Opened wide, wide;
The ship cut softly through the silken surface ;
    We watched white sea-birds ride
Unrocking on the holy virgin water
    Fleckless on every side.

TO ARCTURUS RETURNING

Arcturus, with the spring returning,
    I love you best; I cannot tell
Why, save that your recurrent burning
    Is spring's most punctual miracle.

You bring with you all longed-for things.
    Birds with their song, leaves with their stir.
And you, beyond all other stars.
    Have been man's comforter.

A JUNE DAY

I heard a red-winged black-bird singing
    Down where the river sleeps in the reeds;
That was morning, and at noontime
    A humming-bird flashed on the jewel-weeds;
Clouds blew up, and in the evening
    A yellow sunset struck through the rain.
Then blue night, and the day was ended
    That never will come again.

RHYME OF NOVEMBER STARS

The noiseless marching of the stars
Sweeps above me all night long;
Up the skies, over the skies.
Passes the uncounted throng.
Without haste, without rest.
From the east to the west:
Vega, Deneb, white Altair
Shine like crystals in the air,
And the lonely Fomalhaut
In the dark south, paces low.
Now the timid Pleiades
Leave the shelter of the trees.
While toward the north, mounting high,
Gold Capella, like a queen.
Watches over her demesne
Stretching toward the kingly one,
Dusky, dark Aldebaran.
Betelguese and Rigel burn
In their wide wheel, slow to turn.
And in the sharp November frost
Bright Sirius, with his blue light
Completes the loveliness of night.

I STOOD UPON A STAR

I stretched my mind until I stood
    Out in space, upon a star;
I looked, and saw the flying earth
    Where seven planets are.

Delicately interweaving
    Like fireflies on a moist June night.
The planetoids among the planets
    Played for their own delight.

I watched earth putting off her winter
    And slipping into green;
I saw the dark side of the moon
    No man has ever seen.

Like shining wheels in an opened watch
    They all revolved with soundless motion
Earth sparkled like a rain-wet flower,
    Bearing her petals, plain and ocean.

WINTER NOON

Snow- dust driven over the snow
    In glittering light.
Low hills, far as the eye can go,
    White on white;
Blue as a blue jay, shadows run
    Due north from every tree —
Chipmunk, do you like the sun.
    The blowing snow and me?

MOON'S ENDING

Moon, worn thin to the width of a quill,
    In the dawn clouds flying.
How good to go, light into light, and still
    Giving light, dying.

AUTUMN ON THE BEACHES

Not more blue at the dawn of the world.
    Not more virgin or more gay.
Never in all the million years
    Was the sea happier than to-day.

The sand was not more trackless then,
    Morning more stainless or more cold-
Only the forest and the fields
    Know that the year is old.

AGE

Brooks sing in the spring
    And in summer cease;
I who sang in my youth
    Now hold my peace;
Youth is a noisy stream
    Chattering over the ground,
But the sad wisdom of age
    Wells up without sound.

IN A DARKENING GARDEN

Gather together, against the coming of night.
    All that we played with here.
Toys and fruits, the quill from the sea-bird's flight,
    The small flute, hollow and clear;
The apple that was not eaten, the grapes untasted —
    Let them be put away.
They served for us, I would not have them wasted,
    They lasted out our day.

IN MEMORY OF VACHEL LINDSAY

"Deep in the ages," you said, "deep in the ages,"
    And, "To live in mankind is far more than to live in
        a name."
You are deep in the ages, now, deep in the ages.
    You whom the world could not break, nor the years
name.

Fly out, fly on, eagle that is not forgotten.
    Fly straight to the innermost light, you who loved
        sun in your eyes.
Free of the fret, free of the weight of living.
    Bravest among the brave, gayest among the wise.

GRACE BEFORE SLEEP

How can our minds and bodies be
Grateful enough that we have spent
Here in this generous room, we three,
This evening of content?
Each one of us has walked through storm
And fled the wolves along the road;
But here the hearth is wide and warm.
And for this shelter and this light
Accept, O Lord, our thanks to-night.

LINES

These are the ultimate highlands,
Like chord on chord of music
Climbing to rest
On the highest peak and the bluest
Large on the luminous heavens
Deep in the west.

"THERE WILL BE REST"

There will be rest, and sure stars shining
    Over the roof-tops crowned with snow,
A reign of rest, serene forgetting.
    The music of stillness holy and low.

I will make this world of my devising
    Out of a dream in my lonely mind,
I shall find the crystal of peace,— above me
    Stars I shall find.

www.ingramcontent.com/pod-product-compliance
Lightning Source LLC
Chambersburg PA
CBHW021448080526
44588CB00009B/754